Never Let
a Fool Kiss You or
a Kiss Fool You

Never Let

a Fool Kiss You or

a Kiss Fool You

Chiasmus
and a World of Quotations
That Say What They Mean and
Mean What They Say

DR. MARDY GROTHE

VIKING

VIKING
Published by the Penguin Group
Penguin Putnam Inc., 375 Hudson Street,
New York, New York 10014, U.S.A.
Penguin Books Ltd, 27 Wrights Lane,
London W8 5TZ, England
Penguin Books Australia Ltd, Ringwood,
Victoria, Australia
Penguin Books Canada Ltd, 10 Alcorn Avenue,
Toronto, Ontario, Canada M4V 3B2
Penguin Books (N.Z.) Ltd, 182-190 Wairau Road,
Auckland 10, New Zealand

Penguin Books Ltd, Registered Offices:
Harmondsworth, Middlesex, England

First published in 1999 by Viking Penguin,
a member of Penguin Putnam Inc.

1 3 5 7 9 10 8 6 4 2

"In thigh-high yellow leather boots" by X. J. Kennedy is published by arrangement
with the author. Copyright © 1999
by X. J. Kennedy.

Images from *864 Humorous Cuts from the Twenties and Thirties*,
Dover Publications, Inc. Used by arrangement with the publisher.

LIBRARY OF CONGRESS CATALOGING-IN-PUBLICATION DATA
Grothe, Mardy.
Never let a fool kiss you or a kiss fool you: chiasmus and
a world of quotations that say what they mean and
mean what they say/ Mardy Grothe.
p.   cm.
ISBN 0-670-87827-8
1. Quotations, English.   2. Chiasmus.   I. Title
PN6081.G76   1999
082—dc21   99-18015

This book is printed on acid-free paper.
∞

Printed in the United States of America
Set in Cochin
Designed by Mia Risberg

To many dear friends
with whom I share
a *love* of *language*

&

To my dear wife, Katherine Robinson,
with whom I share
a *language* of *love*

CONTENTS

◆ vii ◆

"Pardon Me, Do You Know What *Chiasmus* Means?"

DO YOU KNOW what *chiasmus* means? Not sure? Not surprising. Most people—even the most literate people—don't. Here's a hint: Mae West used chiasmus in her signature line:

> "It's not the men in my life,
> it's the life in my men."

So did John F. Kennedy in his immortal line:

> "Ask not what your country can do for you,
> ask what you can do for your country."

What do these quotes have in common besides being two of the most memorable lines of the century? Chiasmus (pronounced ky-AZ-mus).

I accidentally stumbled upon the word while browsing

through a dictionary eight years ago and have since discovered that many of the world's great wits, profound thinkers, and eloquent orators—Churchill, Wilde, Shaw, Ben Franklin, Samuel Johnson, and Shakespeare—have been virtual masters of chiasmus. Impressive examples of chiasmus have also come from such moderns as Mark Twain, Will Rogers, Lenny Bruce, Dorothy Parker, and George Carlin. Even Newt Gingrich.

In using chiasmus, these folks are part of a tradition that goes back several thousand years. Chiasmus, you see, is as old as recorded civilization. It shows up in ancient Sanskrit, Mesopotamian, and Egyptian texts. It appears in ancient Chinese writings, including the *Analects* of Confucius. It was an integral feature of ancient Hebrew poetry and is common in both the Old and New Testaments. To the Greeks, though, chiasmus held a special fascination, as Greek sages and orators strove to outdo one anothers' chiastic creations:

"It is not the oath that makes us believe the man,
but the man the oath."
—*Aeschylus* (fifth century B.C.)

"Love as if you would one day hate,
and hate as if you would one day love."
—*Bias* (sixth century B.C.)

"Bad men live that they may eat and drink,
whereas good men eat and drink that they may live."
—*Socrates* (fifth century B.C.)

"One must destroy one's adversaries' seriousness with laughter, and their laughter with seriousness."
— ***Gorgias*** (fourth century B.C.)

What *is* chiasmus? One dictionary defines it this way: A reversal in the order of words in two otherwise parallel phrases. The adjective is *chiastic* (ky-AZ-tick). The *chi* stands for the letter *X* in the Greek alphabet. The word comes from the Greek *khiasmos,* meaning "crossing." And *khiasmos* comes from another Greek word meaning "to mark with an X."

Marking with an X contains the key to grasping the nature of all chiastic quotes. Take the title of this book, which I purloined from Joey Adams. When the clauses are laid out parallel to each other, you can draw two lines connecting the key words:

"Never let a **fool kiss** you

or a **kiss fool** you."

The result is a perfect X. *All* the chiastic quotes in these pages can be marked in this manner. It's a defining feature of chiasmus.

Chiastic quotes can also be displayed in what scholars call an ABBA pattern. Here's how Cicero's famous maxim — based on Socrates' earlier observation — would be laid out:

A	One should *eat*
B	to *live*
B′	not *live*
A′	to *eat*

Chiasmus has gone by many names over the years: inverted parallelism, syntactical inversion, reverse parallelism, crisscross quotes, and turnarounds. William Safire suggested the term *contrapuntal phrases* a few years ago, but it never caught on. Ernest Hemingway, according to friend and biographer A. E. Hotchner, was not familiar with the word *chiasmus*, but was so fascinated with chiastic quotations that he invented his own word to describe them: double *dichos* (from the Spanish *dicho* for "saying"). There are also some tongue-twisting synonyms and related terms, like *antimetabole* and *hysteron proteron*. And while scholars and pedants may quibble over technical differences between these terms, *chiasmus* is the rubric under which they all can comfortably fit.

Chiasmus doesn't involve just the reversal of *words* but also complete *phrases.*

> "Lust is what makes you keep wanting to do it,
> even when you have no desire to be with each other.
> Love is what makes you keep wanting to be with each other,
> even when you have no desire to do it."
> **—Judith Viorst**

Chiasmus can also be achieved by reversing the *letters* and *sounds* of words and even *numbers.*

> "A magician pulls rabbits out of hats.
> An experimental psychologist pulls habits out of rats."
> **—Anonymous**

> "I find Peale appalling
> and Paul appealing."
> **—Adlai Stevenson**

"A lawyer starts life giving $500 worth of law for $5
and ends giving $5 worth for $500."
—*Benjamin H. Brewster*

All the chiastic quotes in this book contain a reversal of two key words or elements. There's also a form of *extended* chiasmus, in which three or more—often many more—words or elements are reversed. A good example, although briefer than most, comes from Genesis 9:6. Here's how chiastic researchers would diagram it:

A	Whoever *sheds*
B	the *blood*
C	of *man*
C′	by *man* shall
B′	his *blood*
A′	be *shed*

Biblical scholars have for many years been intrigued by discoveries of large chiastic passages in the Bible and more recently in the Book of Mormon. Extended chiasmus goes beyond the scope of this book, but no discussion of chiasmus is complete without its being mentioned.

As a literary and rhetorical device, chiasmus has woven itself into the fabric of human life. The greatest speeches of all time would be weaker without chiasmus. What other words could JFK have used to rival his famous "Ask not what your country can do for you" line?

The greatest wits would be a little less witty without it. We wouldn't have Winston Churchill's great riposte to a young member of Parliament who approached the master orator and said, "You heard my talk yesterday. What could I have done to put more fire into my speech?" Churchill replied:

"What you should have done is
to have put your speech into the fire."

Or Dorothy Parker's celebrated reply to a friend who asked why
she hadn't attended a play that featured a character loosely based
on her life:

"I've been too fucking busy,
and vice versa."

For nearly a decade my life has been dominated by chiasmus. In
addition to my formal research, whenever I read a book or newspaper, watch television, or go to a movie, I'm on the lookout. I
now have more than eight thousand chiastic quotes in my collec-
tion. I guess it's fair to say that I didn't just get into chiasmus, chiasmus also got into me.

Even though the phenomenon is pervasive, knowledge of the
word that describes it is rare. I ask almost everybody I meet, "Do
you know what *chiasmus* means?" After eight years I can still
count on one hand the number of people who have correctly an-
swered my question.

My goal now is to bring *chiasmus* out of the closet of obscurity
and share it with a larger audience. Sometimes I even dream of
seeing this unfamiliar word become a part of popular parlance. It
happened once before with a strange and unfamiliar word: *oxy-
moron.* Fifty years ago *it* was an obscure word, known by a small
and select group of people. In the 1950s and 1960s more people
began using it, but it still remained uncommon. In the 1970s and
1980s it surged in popularity, and today virtually all literate people know what it means. I believe the same thing can happen
with *chiasmus,* in my opinion an even more interesting figure of
speech.

Another dream I have is to bring more chiastic quotes into the world, and I'm gratified to report that my work has already inspired some impressive chiastic wordplay. After reading an early version of my manuscript, the noted poet X. J. Kennedy composed a little poem. Here it is, for the first time ever in print:

> "In thigh-high yellow leather boots
> Plump Saphonisba strides.
> Too bad that, just to hide her calves,
> Two calves have lost their hides."

I've organized this anthology of chiastic quotes by topics, and within each topic, alphabetically by the name of those quoted. That way you can quickly scan for quotes from your favorite wit or wordsmith. I've provided a specific author index at the back of the book.

Is this book for you? From the beginning the target audience has been intellectually curious readers with an interest in words, language, and quotations. If you fit this description, you'll know it. I also think the book will have a special appeal to people with a *professional* interest in words and language: writers, poets, public speakers, politicians, speechwriters, CEOs, lawyers, advertising people, preachers, and teachers—especially teachers of English, writing, poetry, and public speaking.

Advance readers have said they found the book most satisfying when they adopted a slow, reflective pace. Chiastic quotes can be very rich and, like all rich things, can be quite filling when too many are consumed in one sitting. You'll probably enjoy the book more if you dip in for many brief tastings, rather than gorge yourself.

I've striven for accuracy, but I'm sure I've made my share of errors. If you discover any mistakes or want to offer any feedback, please feel free to contact me. If you know of a great chiastic quote I have not included, send it my way. And if the book inspires you to craft a chiastic quote or two, I'd be honored if you'd share your creations with me. You can reach me in care of the publisher or via E-mail at: DrMGrothe@aol.com.

And if you find yourself coming down with a case of "chiastic fever," you may find relief by surfing to www.chiasmus.com, the only site on the Web devoted to bringing quotations into your life and life into your quotations.

Welcome to the world of chiasmus.

Never Let

a Fool Kiss You or
a Kiss Fool You

CHAPTER 1

Chiastic Wordplay

CHIASMUS HAS ENJOYED a special place in the hearts of those who have a fascination with words at play. It seems fitting that language maven William Safire should compose a chiastic motto to guide his column-writing efforts:

> "Better a jerk that knees
> than a knee that jerks."

This is chiastic wordplay at its best. Safire couldn't have crafted a better way of saying he'd rather be seen as a dirty fighter than as an ideological automaton.

Arguably the best toast ever created, combining punning with chiasmus, goes all the way back to Edwardian England in the 1890s:

> "Here's champagne for our real friends,
> and real pain for our sham friends."

Nobody appreciated the playful use of language more than famed lexicographer Dr. Samuel Johnson. One of his peers, John Gay, had shopped his play *The Beggar's Opera* around to London theaters, only to have it rejected again and again. Finally he took it to producer John Rich, who saw the play's potential and helped make it a huge success. The legendary wordsmith's comment was soon being repeated all over London:

> "It made Rich gay
> and Gay rich."

More chiastic wordplay follows.

———

"The two greatest highway menaces
are drivers under twenty-five
going over sixty-five
and drivers over sixty-five
going under twenty-five."
—*Anonymous*

"*Beauty* sounds as ugly
as *ugliness* sounds beautiful."
—*Max Beerbohm*

"A scout troop consists of twelve little kids dressed like schmucks
following a big schmuck dressed like a kid."
—*Jack Benny*

"Architect, *n.* One who drafts a plan of your house,
and plans a draft of your money."
—*Ambrose Bierce*

"The gambling known as business
looks with austere disfavor upon
the business known as gambling."
—*Ambrose Bierce*

"You have to know how
to accept rejection
and reject acceptance."
—*Ray Bradbury,*
advice to writers

"In the Halls of Justice
the only justice is in the halls."
—*Lenny Bruce*

"They have to be extra careful with those two-way words.
I mean, they can prick their finger,
but they can't finger their prick."
—*George Carlin,*
on the effect of censors on performers

"Have you noticed that your shit is stuff
and their stuff is shit?"
—*George Carlin*

"Errol Flynn died on a 70-foot boat with a 17-year-old girl.
Walter has always wanted to go that way,
but he's going to settle for a 17-footer with a 70-year-old."
—*Betsy Maxwell Cronkite,*
on husband, Walter

"As a young man I used to have
four supple members and a stiff one.
Now I have four stiff and one supple."
—*Henri-Eugène duc d'Aumale*

"Whether a man's lust for big-breasted women
is a hunger for mountains
or his hunger for mountains is
a lust for big-breasted women is a moot question."
—*Brendan Francis*

"I'd Rather Have a Bottle in Front of Me
(Than a Frontal Lobotomy)."
—*Randy Hanzlick,*
song title

"Man can be destroyed but not defeated.
Man can be defeated but not destroyed."
—*Ernest Hemingway*

"Punctuation is made for man,
not man for punctuation."
—*Philip Howard*

"I don't suffer fools,
and I like to see fools suffer."
—*Florence King*

"Recreational wordplayers wonder why
we drive on a parkway
and park on a driveway."
—*Richard Lederer*

"In what other language do people
play at a recital
and recite at a play?"
—*Richard Lederer,*
on "Crazy English"

"In some parts of Ireland,
the sleep which knows no waking
is always followed by
a wake which knows no sleeping."
—*Mary Wilson Little*

"The telephone is
the greatest nuisance
among conveniences,
the greatest convenience
among nuisances."
—*Robert Lynd*

"In the blue grass region,
A paradox was born:
The corn was full of kernels
And the *colonels* full of corn."
—*John Marshall,*
describing Kentucky

"I despise the pleasure
of pleasing people that I despise."
—*Lady Mary Wortley Montagu*

"The story of the whale swallowing Jonah . . .
borders greatly on the marvelous;
but it would have approached nearer to the idea of miracle
if Jonah had swallowed the whale."
—*Thomas Paine*

"There are painters
who transform the sun into a yellow spot,
but there are others who, thanks to their art and intelligence,
transform a yellow spot into the sun."
—*Pablo Picasso*

"Better a witty fool
than a foolish wit."
—*William Shakespeare*
in *Twelfth Night*

"Don't sweat the petty things
and don't pet the sweaty things."
—*Jacquelyn Small*

"If you talk to God, you are praying;
if God talks to you, you have schizophrenia."
—*Thomas Szasz*

"We usually call our blunders mistakes,
and our friends style our mistakes blunders."
—*Henry Wheatley*

"A monk asks a superior if it is permissible
to smoke while praying.
The superior says certainly not.
Next day, the monk asks the superior if it is permissible
to pray while smoking.
That, says the superior, is not merely permissible, it is admirable."

—*George F. Will*

CHAPTER 2

Chiastic Maxims
to Guide Your Life

IN THE EARLY 1960s, Joseph P. Kennedy told reporters that he had drilled a motto into his sons as they were growing up:

"When the going gets tough,
the tough get going."

The saying has become hackneyed over the years, and even the object of several parodies, but after the Kennedy connection was made, it became internationally famous. Some even began calling it a modern proverb.

Nobody loved a catchy bit of wisdom more than Benjamin Franklin, and nobody did more to popularize the aphorism. Franklin's *Poor Richard's Almanack*, published from 1733 to 1758, was available in all thirteen colonies, eventually selling more than five hundred thousand copies a year, an astonishing figure. Franklin mixed an assortment of practical information on weather, health, and cooking with numerous sayings from a fictional creation by the name of Poor Richard Saunders, a hard-working Quaker weatherman with a shrewish wife named Brigitte. Many of Poor Richard's aphorisms and epigrams were shamelessly lifted—without attribution—from ancient and contemporary European writers. Franklin's *Almanack* helped make familiar many chiastic sayings, including:

> "Keep care of thy shop
> and thy shop will keep care of you."

> "A brother may not be a friend,
> but a friend will always be a brother."

Chiasmus, by capturing meaningful *content* and placing it within an arresting, easy-to-recall *format*, is ideal for creating maxims. But it's up to you to put them into practice."

> "The secret of life is not to do what you like
> but to like what you do."
> —*Anonymous*

> "Never forget what is worth remembering
> or remember what is best forgotten."
> —*Anonymous*

"We should behave to our friends as we
would wish our friends to behave to us."
—*Aristotle*

"Those who mind don't matter,
and those who matter don't mind."
—*Bernard Baruch*

"Judge not,
that you be not judged."
—**The Bible,** Matthew 7:1

"Do not pray for tasks equal to your powers;
pray for powers equal to your tasks."
—*Phillips Brooks*

"If you treat a sick child like an adult
and a sick adult like a child,
everything usually works out pretty well."
—*Ruth Carlisle*

"Half of our mistakes in life arise from
feeling where we ought to think,
and thinking where we ought to feel."
—*John Churton Collins*

"When you have nothing to say,
say nothing."
—*Charles Caleb Colton*

"Don't worry that other people don't know you;
worry that you don't know other people."
—Confucius

"Treat all disasters as if they were trivialities
but never treat a triviality as if it were a disaster."
—Quentin Crisp

"Never be haughty to the humble;
never be humble to the haughty."
—Jefferson Davis

"We're not primarily put on this earth
to see through one another,
but to see one another through."
—Peter De Vries

"Action may not always bring happiness,
but there is no happiness without action."
—Benjamin Disraeli

"Resolve to perform what you ought;
perform without fail what you resolve."
—Benjamin Franklin

"If your religion does not
change you, then you should
change your religion."
—*Elbert Hubbard*

"What we need most is not so much
to realize the ideal
as to idealize the real."
—*Frederic H. Hedge*

"Put not your trust in money,
but put your money in trust."
—*Oliver Wendell Holmes, Sr.*

"We too often love things and use people
when we should be using things and loving people."
—*Reuel L. Howe*

"Try to learn something about everything
and everything about something."
—*Thomas H. Huxley*

"Do what is easy
as if it were difficult,
and what is difficult
as if it were easy."
—*Baltasar Gracián*

KWA PEWRA
STAND BACK
OR GIT
SPLASHED

"It is better to deserve without receiving,
than to receive without deserving."
—*Robert G. Ingersoll*

"If you are idle, be not solitary;
if you are solitary, be not idle."
—*Dr. Samuel Johnson*

"Don't serve time,
let time serve you."
—*Anna M. Kross,*
to Rikers Island inmates

"Defeat the fear of death
and welcome the death of fear."
—*G. Gordon Liddy*

"Treat your friend as if he will one day be your enemy,
and your enemy as if he will one day be your friend."
—*Laberius*

"Never accept flattery as though it were a compliment,
and never treat a compliment as though it were mere flattery."
—*Russell Lynes*

"At a dinner party
one should eat wisely but not too well,
and talk well but not too wisely."
— *W. Somerset Maugham*

"The earth does not belong to man,
man belongs to the earth."
— *Chief Seattle*

"It is best to learn as we go,
not go as we have learned."
— *Leslie Jeanne Sahler*

"Take care to get what you like
or you will be forced to like what you get."
— *George Bernard Shaw*

"Treat your friends like family
and your family like friends."
— *Michele B. Slung,*
citing a "momily" from her mother

"You don't have to be great to start,
but you have to start to be great."
— *Zig Ziglar*

CHAPTER 3

Chiastic Comparisons

HUMAN BEINGS HAVE an almost innate desire to compare and contrast. Too often, though, comparisons have a one-dimensional quality, even when they may be interesting in other ways, as in "Men are from Mars, women are from Venus."

When chiasmus is used to make comparisons, though, something special happens. In the sixth century B.C., the Lydian king Croesus said:

> "In peace, sons bury their fathers;
> in war, fathers bury their sons."

In his 1621 classic on melancholy, Robert Burton described the difference between poor and rich people this way:

> "One is miserably happy,
> the other happily miserable."

And as baby boomers have gotten older, a French proverb—often attributed to Victor Hugo—has enjoyed renewed popularity:

"Forty is the old age of youth;
fifty is the youth of old age."

With a striking economy of words, essential differences are pinpointed and highlighted, often in an unforgettable way. As a result, chiasmus is unrivaled as a vehicle for making comparisons.

———

"Success is getting what you want;
happiness is wanting what you get."
—*Anonymous*

"An optimist goes to the window every morning
and says, 'Good morning, God!'
The pessimist goes to the window every morning
and says, 'Good God! Morning!'"
—*Anonymous*

"The difference between the Scotch and the English
is that the Scotch are hard in all other respects
but soft with women,
and the English are hard with women
and soft in all other respects."
—*J. M. Barrie*

"The error of youth is to believe that
intelligence is a substitute for experience,
while the error of age is to believe that
experience is a substitute for intelligence."
—*Lyman Bryson*

"The manner of a vulgar man
has freedom without ease;
the manner of a gentleman,
ease without freedom."
—*Lord Chesterfield*

"An adventure is only an inconvenience rightly considered.
An inconvenience is only an adventure wrongly considered."
—*G. K. Chesterton*

"Art produces ugly things
which frequently become beautiful with time.
Fashion . . . produces beautiful things
which always become ugly with time."
—*Jean Cocteau*

"A fool often fails because he
thinks what is difficult is easy,
and a wise man because he
thinks what is easy is difficult."
—*John Churton Collins*

"When nature exceeds culture, we have the rustic.
When culture exceeds nature, we have the pedant."
—*Confucius,*
from *Analects,* 6.16

"Friendship is love minus sex and plus reason.
Love is friendship plus sex and minus reason."
—*Mason Cooley*

"Painting is poetry that is seen rather than felt,
and poetry is painting that is felt rather than seen."
—*Leonardo da Vinci*

"There are amusing people who do not interest,
and interesting people who do not amuse."
—*Benjamin Disraeli*

"It is the old story again:
once we had wooden chalices and golden priests,
now we have golden chalices and wooden priests."
—*Ralph Waldo Emerson*

"Stoicism is the wisdom of madness
and cynicism is the madness of wisdom."
—*Bergen Evans*

"Erotic love begins with separateness, and ends in oneness.
Motherly love begins with oneness, and leads to separateness."
—*Erich Fromm*

"In Europe men and women
have intercourse because they love each other.
In the South Seas they
love each other because they have had intercourse.
Who is right?"
—*Paul Gauguin*

"To love is to admire with the heart;
to admire is to love with the mind."
—*Théophile Gautier*

"The pessimist sees the difficulty
in every opportunity;
the optimist, the opportunity
in every difficulty."
—*L. P. Jacks*

"The difference between a well-bred and ill-bred man is this. . . .
You love the one till you find reason to hate him;
you hate the other till you find reason to love him."
—*Dr. Samuel Johnson*

"All misanthropes are curmudgeons,
but all curmudgeons are not misanthropes."
—*Florence King*

"The conventional army loses if it does not win.
The guerrilla wins if he does not lose."
—*Henry A. Kissinger*

"In Plato's opinion man was made for philosophy,
in Bacon's opinion philosophy was made for man."
—*Thomas Babington Macaulay*

"It is the dull man who is always sure,
and the sure man who is always dull."
—*H. L. Mencken*

"Earthly things must be known to be loved;
divine things must be loved to be known."
—*Blaise Pascal*

"A statesman is a politician who
places himself at the service of the nation.
A politician is a statesman who
places the nation at his service."
—*Georges Pompidou*

"A flawed candidate with a strong character
versus a strong candidate with a flawed character."
—*David M. Shribman,*
on Dole and Clinton in 1996

"In Russia religion is the opium of the people,
in China opium is the religion of the people."
—*Edgar Snow,*
on pre-Mao China

"Handel was a man of the world;
but Bach was a world of a man."
—*Arnold Stevenson*

"The first half of life consists of the
capacity to enjoy without the chance;
the last half consists of the
chance without the capacity."
—*Mark Twain*

"Politics is war carried out without bloodshed,
while war is politics carried out with bloodshed."
—*Mao Zedong*

CHAPTER 4

The Battle of the Sexes, Chiasmus Style

VIVE LA DIFFÉRENCE! It seems appropriate that chiasmus, so perfectly constructed for making comparisons, should be put to work to illuminate the gender gap. An Italian proverb captures the age-old tendency to trivialize the major sins of men and magnify the minor ones of women:

> "In man, mortal sins are venial;
> in woman, venial sins are mortal."

The double standard has never been better described.

Sometimes something less than eternal damnation is at stake. This intriguing observation on gender-related shopping habits comes from William Binger:

> "A man is a person who will pay two dollars
> for a one-dollar item he wants.
> A woman will pay one dollar
> for a two-dollar item she doesn't want."

Binger's generalization certainly applies to my situation. I'm for-ever paying more for something because I simply must have it, while my wife is always buying something she doesn't need be-cause it's such a bargain. I don't think we're atypical.

Binger's isn't the only politically incorrect notion you'll find in this chapter, so proceed with caution, or at least with tongue in cheek.

————

"Marriage is the price men pay for sex;
sex is the price women pay for marriage."
—*Anonymous*

"A woman should understand a man
more than she loves him;
a man should love a woman
more than he understands her."
—*Anonymous*

"Man is kind only to be cruel;
woman cruel only to be kind."
—*Minna Antrim*

"Man thinks more than he feels,
woman feels more than she thinks."
—*Earl Barnes*

"A woman's head is always influenced by heart;
but a man's heart by his head."
—*Lady Marguerite Blessington*

"Women eat while they are talking;
men talk while they are eating."
—*Malcolm de Chazal*

"Women deprived of the company of men pine,
men deprived of the company of women become stupid."
—*Anton Chekhov*

"In women pity begets love,
in men love begets pity."
—*John Churton Collins*

"Charm is a woman's strength
just as strength is a man's charm."
—*Havelock Ellis*

"Man begins by making love and ends by loving a woman;
woman begins by loving a man and ends by making love."
—*Remy de Gourmont*

"The desire of the man is for the woman,
but the desire of the woman is for the desire of the man."
—*Germaine de Staël*

"In general, I think it true that
women fuck to love
and men love to fuck."
— *Carrie Fisher*

"In prehistoric times women resembled men,
and men resembled women."
— *Anatole France*

"When a man gets up to speak, people listen, then look.
When a woman gets up, people look;
then if they like what they see, they listen."
— *Pauline Frederick*

"A man has his clothes made to fit him;
a woman makes herself fit her clothes."
— *Edgar Watson Howe*

"There never lived a woman
who did not wish she were a man.
There never lived a man
who wished he were a woman."
— *Edgar Watson Howe*

"Men need sexual fulfillment
in order to respond to a woman emotionally;
women need emotional fulfillment
to respond to a man sexually."
—*Ellen Krieg*

"A man is more faithful and true
to another person's secret than his own;
a woman, on the contrary, keeps
her own secret better than another's."
—*Jean de La Bruyère*

"Males seek power to compensate for loss of connection;
females seek connection to compensate for loss of power."
—*Gary Malmon*

"Indeed, I should say without reservation that
men fear and hate women more than
women fear and hate men."
—*Dr. Karl Menninger*

"After a quarrel between a man and a woman
the man suffers chiefly from the thought that
he has wounded the woman;
the woman suffers from the thought that
she has not wounded the man enough."
—*Friedrich W. Nietzsche*

"A woman worries about the future until she has a husband,
but a man never worries about the future until he has a wife."
—Liselotte Pulver

"To a woman the first kiss is the end of the beginning;
to a man it is the beginning of the end."
—Helen Rowland

"What is most beautiful in virile men
is something feminine;
what is most beautiful in feminine women
is something masculine."
—Susan Sontag

"Why are women . . . so much more interesting to men
than men are to women?"
—Virginia Woolf

CHAPTER 5

Chiastic Compliments and Insults

CHIASMUS HAS PLAYED an important role in the history of praise. Cicero's tribute to a Roman statesman serves as a model more than two thousand years after it was first made:

> "The greatest orator among lawyers,
> the greatest lawyer among orators."

Chiasmus also occupies a prominent place in the history of invective. Historians place Alexander VI high on the list of so-called bad popes, whose scandalous behavior helped spur the Protestant Reformation. Patriarch of the infamous Borgia family, Pope Alexander fathered the ruthless Cesare Borgia. This was a notorious pair: The father was a liar and a hypocrite, the son a master of treachery and intrigue. In 1632 the Dutch writer Jacob Cats captured their twin faces of evil:

"It was said of Pope Alexander VI and of his son . . .
that the father never did what he said,
and the son never said what he did."

Compliments and insults are sometimes embedded in the same chiastic remark, with the insult all the sharper by contrast. In 1960 a group of Protestant ministers headed by Norman Vincent Peale issued a statement opposing the Catholic presidential candidate, John F. Kennedy. An immediate outcry ensued, and Peale resigned from the group, but not before Adlai Stevenson had crafted the best "sound bite" of the campaign, contrasting Peale with his favorite churchman, St. Paul.

"I find Paul appealing
and Peale appalling."

Whether you're puffing up or putting down, these chiastic remarks should inspire.

———

"It's not that he 'bites off more than he can chew' . . .
but he chews more than he bites off."
—*Mrs. Henry Adams,*
on Henry James's writing style

"He made China a part of the world,
and the world a part of China."
—*Anonymous,*
on *Deng Xiaoping*

"Rousseau was the philosopher of the artists
and the artist of the philosophers."
—*Allan Bloom*

"There is a touch of the poet in most revolutionaries—
and a touch of the revolutionary in most poets.
But among revolutionary leaders, the finest poet—
and among poets, the most successful revolutionary leader—
has to be Mao Zedong, who was born 100 years ago today."
—The *Boston Globe,*
in a 1993 editorial

"I have seen many a bear led by a man,
but I never before saw a man led by a bear."
—*Margaret Montgomerie Boswell,*
on her husband's devotion to Dr. Samuel Johnson

"Swans sing before they die—
'twere no bad thing,
Did certain persons die before they sing."
—*Samuel Taylor Coleridge*

"An excellent adage commands that we should
Relate of the dead that alone which is good;
But of the great lord who here lies in lead
We know nothing good but that he is dead."
—*Samuel Taylor Coleridge*

"Let others speak badly or kindly of the great Richelieu,
My prose or verse will never mention him:
He treated me too kindly to be spoken of badly,
He treated me too badly to be spoken of kindly."
—*Pierre Corneille*

"One of them, to repeat an old phrase,
proceeded to write fiction like psychology,
while the other wrote psychology like fiction."
—*Will Durant,*
on Henry and William James

"I have seen many a man
turn his gold into smoke,
but you are the first who
has turned smoke into gold."
—*Queen Elizabeth I,*
to Sir Walter Raleigh,
who introduced tobacco to England

"Plato is philosophy,
and philosophy Plato."
—*Ralph Waldo Emerson*

"He can write funnier than anyone who can write smarter
and smarter than anyone who can write funnier."
—*Mark Feeney,*
on Roy Blount, Jr.

"Your manuscript is both good and original;
but the part that is good is not original,
and the part that is original is not good."
—*Dr. Samuel Johnson,*
to an aspiring writer

"This man I thought had been a Lord among wits;
but, I find, he is only a wit among Lords!"
—*Dr. Samuel Johnson,*
on Lord Chesterfield

"He made football players out of some men,
but I think he's much more proud that
he made men out of some football players."
—*Marie Lombardi,*
on her husband, Vince Lombardi

"No woman has ever so comforted the distressed —
or so distressed the comfortable."
—*Clare Boothe Luce,*
on Eleanor Roosevelt

"He was a rake among scholars,
and a scholar among rakes."
—*Thomas Babington Macaulay,*
on Sir Richard Steele

"There were gentlemen and there were seamen
in the navy of Charles II.
But the seamen were not gentlemen,
and the gentlemen were not seamen."
—*Thomas Babington Macaulay*

"The conformation of his mind was such that
whatever was little seemed to him great,
and whatever was great seemed to him little."
—*Thomas Babington Macaulay,*
on Horace Walpole

"Some men kiss and do not tell . . .
but George Moore told and did not kiss."
—*Susan Mitchell,*
on romantic fabrication

"He defined wit,
and wit defined him."
—*Mark Nicholls,*
on Oscar Wilde

"It was Roosevelt's genius
to treat kings like commoners
and commoners like kings.
And both loved him for it."
—*Gerald Parshall,*
on Franklin D. Roosevelt

"He restored the Bible to its people,
he restored the people to the Bible."
—*Shimon Peres,*
on David Ben-Gurion

"Some agencies have a public affairs office.
NASA is a public affairs office that has an agency."
—*John Pike,*
after the 1986 *Challenger* explosion

"A wit with dunces,
and a dunce with wits."
—*Alexander Pope,*
on Lewis Theobald

"It's hard to think of any among his fellow immortals
as charming as James who were also as good,
or any as good who were also as charming."
— *George Scialabba,*
on William James

"*Seinfeld* can be painfully amusing
and amusingly painful."
— *Tom Shales*

"Everywhere in the world, music enhances a hall,
with one exception:
Carnegie Hall enhances the music."
— *Isaac Stern*

"All his own geese are swans,
as the swans of others are geese."
— *Horace Walpole,*
on Sir Joshua Reynolds

"Of this blest man, let his just praise be given,
Heaven was in him, before he was in heaven."
— *Izaak Walton,*
on Dr. Richard Sibbes

CHAPTER 6

Chiasmus on Stage and Screen

THE THEATRICAL WORLD has produced some of the best chiastic quotations of all time, like Jack Woodford's characterization of the typical plot of Hollywood movies:

> "Boy meets girl;
> girl gets boy into pickle;
> boy gets pickle into girl."

Another, dating to 1747, is practically the Actor's Creed. As Dr. Samuel Johnson observed, upon the opening of the Drury Lane Theatre:

> "We that live to please
> must please to live."

Not surprisingly, actors have also turned to chiasmus for some of their best lines. As the English writer A. E. Housman lay on his deathbed, his physician did everything he could to make him comfortable. Knowing Housman was fond of risqué stories, his doctor told him about a famous Shakespearean actor who'd recently returned to England after a brief stint in Hollywood. A fan asked the actor what he and his colleagues did to pass the time when they weren't making movies. He replied:

> "Well, we spend half our time lying on the sand
> and looking at the stars
> and the other half lying on the stars
> and looking at the sand."

A look of great pleasure came over Housman's face. "Indeed! Very good!" he said, "I shall have to repeat that on the Golden Floor."

———————

> "Forty years ago there was a young Jewish entertainer
> named Al Jolson who was trying to pass as Negro.
> Today there is a young Negro entertainer
> named Sammy Davis who is trying to pass as Jewish."
> —*Goodman Ace*

> "I'm too young to be old
> and too old to be young."
> —*Kathy Bates,*
> in *Fried Green Tomatoes* (1991)

"Many a man owes his success
to his first wife
and his second wife
to his success."
—*Jim Backus*

"I never liked the men I loved,
and I never loved the men I liked."
—*Fanny Brice*

"It's more a case of my life reflecting my movies
than my movies reflecting my life."
—*Francis Ford Coppola*

"When a defining moment comes along,
you define the moment,
or the moment defines you."
—*Kevin Costner,*
in *Tin Cup* (1996)

"There is always something
so delightfully real about what is phony here.
And something so phony about what is real."
—*Noël Coward,*
on life in Tinseltown

"You see an awful lot of smart guys with dumb women,
but you hardly ever see a smart woman with a dumb guy."
— *Clint Eastwood*

"I don't write pictures about tomatoes that eat people.
I write pictures about people who eat tomatoes."
— *Julius Epstein*

"It is easier to get an actor to be a cowboy
than to get a cowboy to be an actor."
— *John Ford*

"It wasn't so much a question of me finishing with movies.
Movies finished with me."
— *Stewart Granger*

"When I am married, I want to be single,
and when I am single, I want to be married."
— *Cary Grant*

"In feature films the director is God;
in documentary films God is the director."
— *Alfred Hitchcock*

"Lloyd always said that in the theatre
a lifetime was a season
and a season a lifetime."
— *Celeste Holm,*
in *All About Eve* (1950)

"A comedian does funny things;
a good comedian does things funny."
— *Buster Keaton*

"They say the movies should be more like life.
I think life should be more like the movies."
— *Myrna Loy*

"Money will not make you happy,
and happy will not make you money."
— *Groucho Marx*

"Animation is not the art of drawings-that-move,
but the art of movements that are drawn."
— *Norman McLaren*

"The stage can be defined
as a place where
Shakespeare murdered Hamlet
and a great many
Hamlets murdered Shakespeare."
— *Robert Morse*

"Before marriage,
a girl has to make love to a man to hold him.
After marriage,
she has to hold him to make love to him."
—Marilyn Monroe

"In the theatre,
a hero is one who believes that all women are ladies,
a villain one who believes that all ladies are women."
—George Jean Nathan

"We used to have actresses
trying to become stars;
now we have stars
trying to become actresses."
—Sir Laurence Olivier

"Its trade . . . is managed by
businessmen pretending to be artists and by
artists pretending to be businessmen."
—J. B. Priestley,
on Hollywood

"As a director, I wouldn't like me as an actor.
As an actor, I wouldn't like me as a director."
—Robert Redford

"Suit the action to the word,
the word to the action."
—*William Shakespeare,*
Hamlet's instructions to the players

"Love the art in yourself,
not yourself in the art."
—*Konstantin Stanislavsky*

"It's true that gentlemen prefer blondes.
Is it possible that blondes also prefer gentlemen?"
—*Mamie Van Doren,*
in *Gentlemen Prefer Blondes* (1953)

"Jungle people fight to live;
civilized people live to fight."
—*Johnny Weissmuller,*
in *Tarzan Triumphs* (1943)

"It is better to be looked over
than overlooked."
—*Mae West,*
in *Belle of the Nineties* (1934)

"I always say, keep a diary and
someday it'll keep you."
—*Mae West,*
in *Every Day's a Holiday* (1937)

"I wouldn't say when you've seen one Western
you've seen the lot;
but when you've seen the lot
you get the feeling you've seen one."
—*Katharine Whitehorn*

"Hollywood didn't kill Marilyn Monroe;
it's the Marilyn Monroes who are killing Hollywood."
—*Billy Wilder*

"Stars don't make movies,
movies make stars."
—*Darryl F. Zanuck*

CHAPTER 7

Political Chiasmus

CHIASMUS HAS A long and distinguished history in political oratory, but its finest moment came on a cold, clear January morning in 1961. John F. Kennedy, the first Catholic and the youngest person ever elected U.S. president, stepped onto the world stage and delivered one of the greatest inaugural addresses of all time. Kennedy's eloquence, especially his most famous line, stirred the souls of millions:

> "And so, my fellow Americans,
> ask not what your country can do for you,
> ask what you can do for your country."

JFK used chiasmus more effectively than any political figure in history (his inaugural speech featured another well-known chiastic construction: "Let us never negotiate out of fear; but let us never fear to negotiate"). However, JFK's immortal "Ask not" line was not completely original and most likely grew out of seventy-five years of similar chiastic sentiments. The first step on the quote trail takes us to 1916, when Warren G. Harding said at the Republican National Convention:

"In the great fulfillment we must have a citizenship
less concerned about what the government can do for it
and more anxious about what it can do for the nation."

Harding's words in turn may have been inspired by a popular turn-of-the-century writing professor at Harvard, Le Baron Russell Briggs, who wrote in 1904:

"As has often been said,
the youth who loves his Alma Mater will always ask, not
'What can she do for me?' but 'What can I do for her?'"

Briggs suggests the chiastic phrase was not his but was well known. The ultimate source was probably an 1884 speech by Supreme Court Justice Oliver Wendell Holmes, Jr., in which he said:

"It is now the moment when by common consent we pause
to become conscious of our national life and to rejoice in it,
to recall what our country has done for each of us,
and to ask ourselves what we can do for our country in return."

Kennedy, as it turns out, didn't say it first; he simply said it best.

"The man who goes into politics
as a business
has no business
going into politics."
—*Anonymous*

"Just as a strong America means a safer world,
we have learned that a safer world means a stronger America."
—*George Bush*

"America did not invent human rights.
In a very real sense . . . human rights invented America."
—*Jimmy Carter*

"Some men change their party for the sake of their principles;
others their principles for the sake of their party."
—*Winston Churchill*

"It is not enough to preach about family values,
we must value families."
—*Hillary Rodham Clinton*

"As we have throughout this century,
we will lead with the power of our example,
but be prepared, when necessary,
to make an example of our power."
—*Bill Clinton*

"Until recently people thought of the NRA as a
hunting and sporting group that did a little lobbying
on the side. Now it's thought of as a lobbying group
that does a little hunting and sporting on the side."
—*Osha Gray Davidson*

"A government that seizes control of the economy
for the good of the people,
ends up seizing control of the people
for the good of the economy."
—*Robert Dole*

"Political freedom cannot exist in any land
where religion controls the state,
and religious freedom cannot exist in any land
where the state controls religion."
—*Sam Ervin, Jr.*

"We're prepared to place our trust in
the people to reshape the government.
Our liberal friends place their trust in
the government to reshape the people."
—*Newt Gingrich*

"You can commit a crime that's not an impeachable offense,
and you can commit an impeachable offense that's not a crime."
—*Jeff Greenfield,*
during the 1998 impeachment debate

"If government is in the hands of a few
they will tyrannize the many;
if in the hands of the many, they
will tyrannize the few.
It ought to be in the hands of both,
and they should be separated."
—*Alexander Hamilton*

"I have said to the people we mean
to have less government in business
as well as more business in government."
—*Warren G. Harding*

"This is about principled compromise,
not compromised principles."
—*John Hume,*
on Ireland's 1998 Good Friday peace accord

"It is not the function of our Government
to keep the citizen from falling into error;
it is the function of the citizen
to keep the Government from falling into error."
—*Robert H. Jackson,*
in a 1950 Supreme Court opinion

"Were it left to me to decide
whether we should have
a government without newspapers,
or newspapers without a government,
I should not hesitate for a moment
to prefer the latter."
—*Thomas Jefferson*

"It's probably better to have him
inside the tent pissing out,
than outside the tent pissing in."
—*Lyndon B. Johnson,*
on J. Edgar Hoover

"We don't believe in an America that
pursues equality by making rich people poor,
but by allowing poor people, indeed all people, to become rich."
—*Jack Kemp*

"Mankind must put an end to war
or war will put an end to mankind."
—John F. Kennedy

"If more politicians knew poetry, and more poets knew politics,
I am convinced the world would be a little better place to live."
—John F. Kennedy

"A politician wouldn't dream of being allowed to call a columnist
the things a columnist is allowed to call a politician."
—Max Lerner

"It is true that you may fool all the people some of the time;
you can even fool some of the people all the time;
but you can't fool all of the people all the time."
—Abraham Lincoln

"It has been said of the world's history hitherto
that might makes right.
It is for us and for our time to reverse the maxim,
and to say that right makes might."
—Abraham Lincoln

"There is no certain harm in turning a politician into a judge.
He may be or become a good judge.
The curse of the elective system is the converse,
that it turns almost every judge into a politician."
—Henry T. Lummus,
on electing judges

"As a man is said to have a right to his property,
he may be equally said to have a property in his rights."
—*James Madison*

"Most of us are honest all the time,
and all of us are honest most of the time."
—*Charles M. Mathias, Jr.,*
on members of Congress

"In the infancy of societies,
the chiefs of state shape its institutions;
later the institutions shape the chiefs of state."
—*Baron de Montesquieu*

"The conservative leader often has to choose between
those who are loyal and not bright
and those who are bright but not loyal."
—*Richard M. Nixon*

"Nations do not mistrust
each other because they are armed;
they are armed because
they mistrust each other."
—*Ronald Reagan*

"With Congress—every time they make a joke it's a law.
And every time they make a law it's a joke."
— *Will Rogers*

"We cannot always build the future for our youth,
but we can build our youth for the future."
—*Franklin D. Roosevelt*

"The Constitution was made for the people
and not the people for the Constitution."
— *Theodore Roosevelt*

"Speaker Newt Gingrich says
that what is wrong with the present system
is not that people abuse welfare
but that welfare abuses people."
—*Daniel Schorr*

"Here is one instance in which it is
the man who makes the office,
not the office the man."
—*Harry S. Truman,*
on the vice presidency

"I would rather lose in a cause that will some day win,
than win in a cause that will some day lose!"
—*Woodrow Wilson*

CHAPTER 8

Chiasmus in the World of Sports

IN 1905 BASEBALL'S owners commissioned a group to investigate the origins of baseball. After three years of so-called study, and primarily on the basis of an unsubstantiated letter from an elderly man of doubtful sanity, they declared that Abner Doubleday had invented the game of baseball in 1839 in Cooperstown, New York. While historians have totally discredited the claim — for example, Doubleday's own obituary says he disliked outdoor sports — the myth lives on. In his 1973 book *The Man Who Invented Baseball*, Harold Peterson put a chiastic spin on the story:

> "Abner Doubleday didn't invent baseball.
> Baseball invented Abner Doubleday."

Chiasmus is an integral part of the sports world. In addition to the ubiquitous "When the going gets tough" saying, athletes from peewee leagues to the pros have been barraged with chiastic exhortations:

"Winners never quit
and quitters never win."

"Failing to prepare
is preparing to fail."

Every sport has inspired great chiastic lines as well.

———————

"All great horses are fast,
but not all fast horses are great."
—Anonymous horse-racing maxim

"Rugby is a beastly game
played by gentlemen;
soccer is a gentleman's game
played by beasts."
—Henry Blaha

"Joe Schultz would have been a better manager
if he understood more. Of course, if he understood more,
he might not have been a manager."
—Jim Bouton,
on the Seattle Pilots manager Joe Schultz

"We get baseball weather in football season
and football weather in baseball season."
—Herb Caen,
on San Francisco's climate

"A championship team without a sure Hall of Famer
had added a sure Hall of Famer without a championship."
—Gerry Callahan,
on the New York Yankees acquiring Roger Clemens

"It's always the same. Either it's rainy with sunny intervals,
or sunny with rainy intervals."
—Pat DuPre,
on Wimbledon weather

"I've seen a lot more cowboys hurt by the stock
than stock hurt by the cowboys."
—Ken Ferrasci,
on rodeo's alleged cruelty to animals

"It's not the size of the dog in the fight,
it's the size of the fight in the dog."
—Archie Griffith

"The course is playing the players instead of
the players playing the course."
—Walter Hagen,
at 1951 U.S. Open

"I can think of more pitchers that
have been seriously hurt by batted balls
than I can of batters that have been hurt by pitched balls."
—Kirby Higbe,
on the danger of the brushback pitch

"I spent twelve years training for a career
that was over in a week.
Joe spent one week training for a career
that lasted twelve years."
—*Bruce Jenner,*
comparing his and Joe Namath's career

"Let the mind control the body,
not the body control the mind."
—*Jimmy Johnson*

"A ballplayer could go to college and be a sportswriter.
But what writer could be a ballplayer?"
—*Billy Martin*

"I'm not the manager because I'm always right,
but I'm always right because I'm the manager."
Gene Mauch

"There are some fielders
who make the impossible catch
look ordinary
and some the ordinary catch
look impossible."
—*Joe McCarthy*

"To finish first
you must first finish."
—*Rick Mears*

"Throw high risers at the chin;
throw peas at the knees;
throw it here when they're lookin' there;
throw it there when they're lookin' here."
—*Leroy ("Satchel") Paige,*
on how to pitch

"He can beat your'n with his'n
and he can beat his'n with your'n."
— *"Bum" Phillips,*
on Don Shula

"Boys would be big leaguers, as everybody knows,
but so would big leaguers be boys."
—*Philip Roth*

"I am a victim of circumference.
When I stand close enough to the ball to reach it, I can't see it.
When I see it, I can't reach it."
—*Bernard ("Toots") Shor,*
on his golf swing

"In the 70's I threw in the 90's;
in the 90's I throw in the 70's."
—*Frank Tanana,*
on pitching velocity

"Most people don't understand catchers . . .
Jerry Grote is a catcher who hits.
Johnny Bench is a hitter who catches.
There is a big difference."
—Joe Torre

"Golfers find it a very trying matter to turn at the waist,
more particularly if they have a lot of waist to turn."
—Harry Vardon

"The difference between soccer and baseball is that
in baseball you have a father taking his son
and explaining the strategy, and in soccer you have
the son taking his father and explaining it to him."
—Danny Villanueva

"You learn very little
about golf from life,
but you learn a lot
about life from golf."
—Earl Woods,
father of Tiger Woods

"Baseball is too much of a sport to be a business
and too much of a business to be a sport."
—Philip K. Wrigley

CHAPTER 9

Chiasmus in Advertising

FOR MANY YEARS Bernice Fitzgibbons was the director of advertising at Macy's department store in New York City. In her 1967 autobiography, *Macy's, Gimbels & Me*, she borrowed a chiastic sentiment from American writer Finley Peter Dunne when she wrote:

> "A good ad should be like a good sermon;
> it must not only comfort the afflicted,
> it also must afflict the comfortable."

In attempting to arrest the attention of fickle consumers, advertising copywriters have long turned to chiasmus. It's not surprising that a chiastic slogan heralded the arrival of Apple's new iMac computer:

> "Simply Amazing.
> Amazingly Simple."

A few years ago Boston's WGBH-TV featured New Age guru Dr. Deepak Chopra and legendary chef Julia Child in two back-to-back programs. A newspaper ad promoted this unlikely lineup with a neat chiastic connection:

"Food for Thought,
Thought for Food."

Politics is another arena where chiastic slogans thrive. In 1947 Winston Churchill gave a speech at the Al Smith Memorial in New York City. He recalled:

"I had followed Al Smith's contest for the Presidency with keen interest and sympathy . . . I even suggested to him a slogan: 'All for Al and Al for All.'"

Take note, Al Gore.

———

"Everything for the horse except the rider
and everything for the rider except the horse."
—Slogan for Mark Cross leather shops

"A crazy trend
or a trendy craze."
—Slogan for Coffee Coolatta by Dunkin' Donuts

"Fly to the seafood instead of
having the seafood fly to you."
—Slogan for Southwest Airlines East Coast service

"Is it the kids that make the clothes look good,
or the clothes that make the kids look good?"
—Slogan for Oshkosh B'Gosh children's clothes

"Is what you drive
a reflection of who you are?
Or is who you are
a reflection of what you drive?"
—Slogan for Oldsmobile Aurora

"You like it.
It likes you."
—Slogan for Seven-Up

"Is it a home phone that acts like a cellular phone?
Or is it a cellular phone that acts like a home phone?"
—Slogan for Motorola FreedomPlus phone

"Effective people don't just do things differently . . .
they do different things."
—Slogan for Covey Leadership Center

"Your lifetime of experience may become
their experience of a lifetime."
—Slogan urging senior citizens to
mentor younger people

"If guns are outlawed,
only outlaws will have guns."
—Unofficial slogan of the National Rifle Association

"Everything fits into it,
and it fits into everything."
—Slogan for Volkswagen Golf

"Drive one not to escape life.
But to prevent life from escaping you."
—Slogan for BMW's Z3 convertible

"You always had time for coffee.
Now your coffee has time for you."
—Slogan for coffee mug with a built-in clock

"History through the eyes of Harts and
Harts through the eyes of History."
—Slogan for *Hart Historical Notes* newsletter

"Shop where you bank.
Bank where you shop."
—Slogan for BankBoston's supermarket locations

"What Chicago makes,
makes Chicago."
—Slogan for Chicago Chamber of Commerce

"The best way to do
business in America
may be to have a little more
America in your business."
—Slogan by Ad Club of Boston
promoting diversity in hiring

"It's not what you're eating,
it's what's eating you."
—Slogan for Dr. Janet Greeson's diet program

"Live to Ride,
Ride to Live."
—Slogan for Harley-Davidson motorcycles

"We're not better because we're bigger,
we're bigger because we're better."
—Slogan for Filter Fresh Coffee

"I lease the car,
the car doesn't lease me."
—Slogan for Chevrolet's Smart Lease Program

"It's not the food in your life,
but the life in your food that really counts."
—Slogan for "The Juiceman," Jay Kordich

An ad for the Boston Public Library featured a picture of a tough-looking "biker" type—complete with leather motorcycle jacket and bushy moustache—totally engrossed in a book, *The Collected Poems of Emily Dickinson.* The caption said:

"When you read a book,
it changes the way you look at the world
and the way the world looks at you."

CHAPTER 10

Chiasmus for CEOs

CONFUCIUS SPENT MOST of his life looking for a Chinese prince who would heed his thoughts about how to govern. He never found one, causing Will Durant to call him "the sage in search of a state." Advancing in years, he began teaching students instead. Many of his students went on to become government officials and advisers, thus helping the sage—posthumously— achieve his lifelong dream. For two thousand years Chinese rulers studied such chiastic Confucian thoughts as:

"Advance the honest over the crooked,
and the people will be loyal.
Advance the crooked over the honest,
and the people will be disloyal."

Throughout history, leaders in training have been guided by chiastic sayings. In ancient India, sons and daughters of royalty were schooled in leadership by reading a book of animal fables called *The Panchatantra.* One typical lesson concluded:

> "Better have as king a vulture advised by swans
> than a swan advised by vultures."

Powerful leaders have themselves created powerful chiastic sayings. Chabrias, the brilliant Greek military leader, twice led Athenian troops to victory over the Spartans. Greek rulers—as well as the kings of Egypt and Cyprus, who sought his help to defeat their enemies—were mindful of his immodest remark:

> "An army of stags led by a lion
> is more to be feared than
> an army of lions led by a stag."

Like leaders of the past, today's CEOs are often inspired by chiastic quotations. One of the most impressive businessmen I know says he became successful only after overcoming a lifelong problem: a tendency to talk too much and listen too little. His secret? Before every meeting—with employees and customers—he silently reminded himself:

> "People don't care how much you know
> until they know how much you care."

If you're a CEO—or a CEO aspirant—here's more chiastic wisdom to chew on.

"People are known by the company they keep;
companies are known by the people they keep."
—*Anonymous*

"The person who is too big for a small job
is too small for a big job."
—*Anonymous*

"When buyers don't fall for prices,
prices must fall for buyers."
—*Anonymous*

"The two biggest problems in corporate America
are making ends meet
and making meetings end."
—*Anonymous*

"Think like a man of action,
act like a man of thought."
—*Henri Bergson*

"It is more difficult . . . to rule the King's favorites
than for the favorites to rule the King."
—*Marjorie Bowen*

"I am a better investor because I am a businessman,
and I am a better businessman because I am an investor."
—*Warren Buffett*

"If we command our wealth, we shall be rich and free;
if our wealth commands us, we are poor indeed."
—*Edmund Burke*

"I do not hold with those who say
that power corrupts men.
Rather, it is the other way around;
men without morality corrupt power."
—*Arthur Burns*

"Take away my people, but leave my factories,
and soon grass will grow on the factory floors.
Take away my factories, but leave my people,
and soon we will have a new and better factory."
—*Andrew Carnegie*

"Natural ability without education
has more often raised a man to
glory and virtue than
education without natural ability."
—*Cicero*

"The superior man is easy to serve, but difficult to please . . .
The inferior man is difficult to serve, but easy to please."
—*Confucius*

"Nothing so soon the drooping spirits can raise
As praises from the men, whom all men praise."
—*Abraham Cowley*

"He that makes his pleasure be his business,
will never make his business be a pleasure."
—*Daniel Defoe*

"Never shrink from anything
which your business calls you to do.
The man who is
above his business
may one day find
his business above him."
—*Daniel Drew*

"Management is doing things right;
leadership is doing the right things."
—*Peter F. Drucker*

"It is difficult for a rich person to be modest,
or a modest person to be rich."
—*Epictetus*

"As a madman is apt to think
himself grown suddenly great,
so he that grows suddenly great
is apt to borrow a little from the madman."
 —*Dr. Samuel Johnson*

"It is better to debate a question without deciding it
than to decide it without debating it."
 —*Joseph Joubert*

"The man who thinks he can do without the world
is indeed mistaken;
the man who thinks the world cannot do without him
is mistaken even worse."
 —*François de La Rochefoucauld*

"Money never starts an idea.
It is always the idea that
starts the money."
 —*Owen Laughlin*

"He once said that all readers can't be leaders,
but all leaders must be readers."
 —*David McCullough,*
of Harry Truman

"Show me the leader and I will know his men.
Show me the men and I will know their leader."
—*Arthur W. Newcomb*

"In one case out of a hundred
a point is excessively discussed because it is obscure;
in the ninety-nine remaining
it is obscure because it is excessively discussed."
—*Edgar Allan Poe*

"If you suspect a man, don't employ him,
and if you employ him, don't suspect him."
—*Proverb* (Chinese)

"A friendship founded on business
is better than
a business founded on friendship."
—*John D. Rockefeller, Jr.*

"It isn't enough for you to love money—
it's also necessary that money should love you."
—*Baron Nathan Rothschild*

"Happy is the time where the great listen to the small,
for in such a generation the small will listen to the great."
—*The Talmud*

"It is better to deserve honors and not have them than to have them and not deserve them."
—*Mark Twain*

"Money sometimes makes fools of important persons, but it may also make important persons of fools."
—*Walter Winchell*

"Don't wait until you feel like taking a positive action. Take the action and then you will feel like doing it."
—*Zig Ziglar*

CHAPTER 11

Chiasmus for Book Lovers

IN THE NINETEENTH century, the life of the French writer George Sand had all the trappings of a real page-turner. After an unexceptional youth, she broke out of an unsatisfying marriage, acquired a series of lovers (including the poet Alfred de Musset and the composer Frederic Chopin), took up some audacious habits (she not only assumed a male pseudonym, but also dressed as a man and smoked cigars), and began a successful writing career that featured heroines who spurned stifling social conventions. When Sand dumped Musset for another man, he became so angry that he wrote a pornographic novel featuring a thinly veiled version of her. Sand was writing from a wealth of experience when she penned this memorable line:

"Life resembles a novel more often
than novels resemble life."

In modern times, confessional literature has become so much the norm that no one knows where to draw the line. In Philip Roth's

1990 novel *Deception,* one of his characters conveys the exasperation that Roth himself has undoubtedly felt over the years:

> "I write fiction and I'm told it's autobiography,
> I write autobiography and I'm told it's fiction."

Mark Twain, however, knew where he stood, firmly on the side of fiction:

> "Some people lie when they tell the truth.
> I tell the truth lying."

In this chapter, writers use chiasmus to describe themselves, their craft, and the essence of the literary life.

———

"In the case of good books,
the point is not to see
how many of them
you can get through,
but rather how many
can get through to you."
—*Mortimer J. Adler*

"In poetry you have a form looking for a subject
and a subject looking for a form.
When they come together successfully you have a poem."
— *W. H. Auden*

"It is well to read everything of something,
and something of everything."
—*Henry Brougham*

"The original writer is not one who imitates nobody,
but one whom nobody can imitate."
—*François René de Chateaubriand*

"The function of the imagination is
not to make strange things settled,
so much as to make settled things strange."
—*G. K. Chesterton*

"There is a great deal of difference between
the eager man who wants to read a book
and the tired man who wants a book to read."
—*G. K. Chesterton*

"Sit down to write what you have thought
and not to think about what you shall write."
—*William Cobbett*

"What is style?
For many people, a very complicated way
of saying very simple things.
According to us, a very simple way
of saying very complicated things."
—*Jean Cocteau*

"It may be possible in novel-writing
to present characters successfully without telling a story;
but it is not possible
to tell a story successfully without presenting characters."
—*Wilkie Collins*

"Better to write for yourself and have no public,
than to write for the public and have no self."
—*Cyril Connolly*

"I do not 'get' ideas;
ideas get me."
—*Robertson Davies*

"The secret of good writing is
to say an old thing in a new way
or to say a new thing an old way."
—*Richard Harding Davis*

"Only after the writer lets literature shape her
can she perhaps shape literature."
—Annie Dillard

"The bad poet is usually
unconscious where he ought to be conscious,
and conscious where he ought to be unconscious."
—T. S. Eliot

"Words are also actions,
and actions are a kind of words."
—Ralph Waldo Emerson

"You don't write because you want to say something;
you write because you've got something to say."
—F. Scott Fitzgerald

"There are, in actual fact,
men who talk like books.
Happily, however, there are also
books that talk like men."
—Theodor Haecker

"The book-lover needs most to be reminded
that man's business here is to know for the sake of living,
not to live for the sake of knowing."
—Frederic Harrison

"It is the business of reviewers to watch poets,
not of poets to watch reviewers."
— *William Hazlitt*

"I began to get an idea: to write a book that
explained the principles of Taoism
through Winnie-the-Pooh,
and explained Winnie-the-Pooh
through the principles of Taoism."
— *Benjamin Hoff,*
on the 1992 book *The Tao of Pooh*

"Tell him that some men are more interesting than their books
but my book is more interesting than its man."
— *A. E. Housman,*
rejecting a request for an interview

"The two most engaging powers of an author are
to make new things familiar,
and familiar things new."
— *Dr. Samuel Johnson*

"This isn't a bar for writers with a drinking problem,
it's for drinkers with a writing problem."
— *Judy Joice,*
on The Lion's Head, a Greenwich Village writers' haunt

"It is not Goethe who creates 'Faust'
but 'Faust' which creates Goethe."
— *Carl Jung*

"I drink because I'm unhappy.
Just then, I shifted the equation, rearranged the words:
Maybe, just maybe, I'm unhappy because I drink."
—*Caroline Knapp,*
from *Drinking: A Love Story*

"I can write better than
anybody who can write faster,
and I can write faster than
anybody who can write better."
—*A. J. Liebling*

"Most people ignore most poetry
because
most poetry ignores most people."
—*Adrian Mitchell*

"You have to look at a novel or a story . . . as saying
something about life colored by the writer,
not about the writer colored by life."
—*Flannery O'Connor*

"I shall live badly if I do not write,
and I shall write badly if I do not live."
—*Françoise Sagan*

"The poet's eye, in a fine frenzy rolling,
Doth glance from heaven to earth,
from earth to heaven."
    — *William Shakespeare*

"Poetry is the record of the best and happiest moments
of the happiest and best minds."
    — *Percy Bysshe Shelley*

"A critic is a necessary evil,
and criticism is an evil necessity."
    — *Carolyn Wells*

"For the friends life has given me,
and for the life friends have given me."
    — *Lois Wyse,*
dedicating her 1996 book
Women Make the Best Friends

CHAPTER 12

Chiasmus for Lovers

GETTING TO THE heart of the matter has been difficult in matters of the heart, since the dynamics of love are often counterintuitive. Two thousand years ago, the Roman poet Ovid wrote *The Art of Love*, the first how-to book on the psychology of love and the art of seduction. Looking to his own experience, Ovid reflected:

> "I flee who chases me,
> and chase who flees me."

As centuries passed, countless writers piggybacked on Ovid's observation. By 1670, when John Ray published his popular book of English proverbs, Ovid's chiastic insight had evolved into a full-fledged proverbial truth:

> "Follow love and it will flee;
> Flee love and it will follow thee."

Chiasmus has a special ability to illuminate not-so-obvious romantic truths. In 1836 the English poet Henry Taylor reflected on the art of courtship. A man of classical learning, he recalled the allure of the sirens of Greek mythology—those enchanting sea goddesses who sang such irresistible songs that sailors passing by felt compelled to get closer, only to perish on the treacherous rocks near the shore. (In Homer's *Odyssey,* Odysseus evades their fatal charms by plugging the ears of his crew and chaining himself to the masthead.) Taylor's words remind suitors that good listening—not fancy talking—is the best way to a woman's heart:

"No siren did ever so charm the ear of the listener
as the listening ear has charmed the soul of the siren."

Chiasmus has helped many other observers of the human scene capture the subtle, intricate, and often paradoxical dynamics of sex, love, and romance.

———

"May we kiss who we please,
and please who we kiss."
—*Anonymous toast*

"Love makes sex better,
sex makes love better."
—*Anonymous*

"Love turns one person into two;
and two into one."
—*Isaac Abravanel*

"Man can start with aversion and end with love,
but if he begins with love and comes round to aversion
he will never get back to love."
—*Honoré de Balzac*

"Youth is unhappy because it is faced with this terrible choice:
Love without peace, or peace without love."
—*Pierre de Beaumarchais*

"Love is the business of the idle,
but the idleness of the busy."
—*Edward George Bulwer-Lytton*

"You can give without loving,
but you cannot love without giving."
—*Amy Wilson Carmichael*

"You can love a person deeply and sincerely
whom you do not like.
You can like a person passionately
whom you do not love."
—*Robert Hugh Benson*

"It is obviously quite difficult to be no longer loved
when we are still in love,
but it is incomparably more painful to be still loved
when we ourselves no longer love."
—*Georges Courteline*

"We must begin to love
in order that we may not fall ill,
and we must fall ill if,
in consequence of frustration,
we cannot love."
—*Sigmund Freud*

"Infantile love follows the principle: 'I love because I am loved.'
Mature love follows the principle: 'I am loved because I love.'
Immature love says: 'I love you because I need you.'
Mature love says: 'I need you because I love you.'"
—*Erich Fromm*

"If you are willing to forget that
there is an element of duty in love
and of love in duty,
then it's easy to choose between the two."
—*Jean Giraudoux*

"When you love you should not say, 'God is in my heart,'
but rather, 'I am in the heart of God.'
And think not you can direct the course of love,
for love, if it finds you worthy, directs your course."
—*Kahlil Gibran*

"Do I love you because you're beautiful?
Or are you beautiful because I love you?"
—*Oscar Hammerstein II,*
from 1957 song "Do I Love You Because You're Beautiful?"

"Love makes time pass,
time makes love pass."
—*Victor Hugo*

"Love is the wisdom of fools
and the folly of the wise."
—*Dr. Samuel Johnson*

"The question is not whether
we have sex desire,
but whether sex desire has us."
—*E. Stanley Jones*

"Where love rules, there is no will to power;
and where power predominates, there love is lacking."
—*Carl Jung*

"A wise lover values not so much the gift of the lover
as the love of the giver."
—*Thomas à Kempis*

Joy is not a substitute for sex,
sex is very often a substitute for Joy."
—*C. S. Lewis*

"It is fairly easy to find a mistress,
and it is not at all difficult to hold on to a friend.
What is hard, is to find a friend
and to hold on to a mistress."
—*Gaston Pierre Marc, Duc de Lévis*

"We don't love a woman for what she says,
but we like what she says because we love her."
—*André Maurois*

"You mustn't force sex to do the work of love
or love to do the work of sex."
—*Mary McCarthy*

"Without love intelligence is dangerous;
without intelligence love is not enough."
—*Ashley Montagu*

"Age doesn't protect you from love.
But love, to some extent, protects you from age."
—*Jeanne Moreau*

"A friend is one who loves you;
but one who loves you isn't necessarily your friend."
—*Seneca the Younger*

"O powerful love,
that in some respects makes a beast a man,
in some other, a man a beast."
—*William Shakespeare,*
in *The Merry Wives of Windsor*

"They say all lovers swear more performance than they are able,
and yet reserve an ability that they never perform."
—*William Shakespeare,*
in *Troilus and Cressida*

"When pain has been intertwined with love and closeness,
it's very difficult to believe that
love and closeness can be experienced without pain."
—*Gloria Steinem*

"If you can't be with the one you love,
love the one you're with."
—*Stephen Stills*,
from 1970 song "Love the One You're With"

"When you are in love you are not wise, or rather,
when you are wise you are not in love."
—*Publilius Syrus*

"I know the nature of women:
when you want to,
they don't want to;
and when you don't want to,
they want to . . . exceedingly."
—*Terence*

"Lust is what makes you keep wanting to do it,
even when you have no desire to be with each other.
Love is what makes you keep wanting to be with each other,
even when you have no desire to do it."
—*Judith Viorst*

"Someone once remarked that
in adolescence pornography is a substitute for sex,
whereas in adulthood sex is a substitute for pornography."
—*Edmund White*,
paraphrasing Edward Albee

"Whereas a lot of men used to ask for conversation
when they really wanted sex,
nowadays they often feel obliged to ask for sex
even when they really want conversation."
—*Katharine Whitehorn*

"We always believe our first love is our last,
and our last love is our first."
—*George Whyte-Melville*

"Is this not the true romantic feeling—
not to desire to escape life,
but to prevent life from escaping you?"
—*Thomas Wolfe*

CHAPTER 13

Chiasmus in Marriage
and Family Life

In THE FIFTH century b.c., Themistocles was one of the most powerful men in Athens. One day his daughter came to him, torn between two marriage proposals. One suitor, she said, had great strength of character but was of limited means. The other was wealthy, and of the same social class as her father, but was of somewhat questionable character. Given the love of the Greeks for chiasmus, her father's unhesitating answer is not surprising:

> "I choose a man without money
> rather than money without a man."

Chiasmus is also well suited for describing the little absurdities of family life. A high-level political adviser in the Clinton administration spent the greater part of one Friday in a series of meetings at the White House debating whether or not to send American troops to Bosnia. That evening he arrived home to discover that his wife and two children had barred him from any role in choosing the videos they were going to rent for the weekend. Truly, then, according to a time-honored saying:

> "Home is where
> the great are small
> and the small are great."

You may recognize aspects of your family — and your family may recognize aspects of you — in the quotes that follow.

———

> "To marry without love
> betrays as surely as
> to love without marriage."
> —*Louisa May Alcott*

> "It begins when you sink in his arms.
> It ends with your arms in his sink."
> —*Anonymous*,
> on marriage

> "Marry for love and you divorce for money;
> marry for money and you divorce for love."
> —*Anonymous*

"I know one husband and wife who, whatever the official
reasons given to the court for the breakup of their marriage,
were really divorced because the husband believed
that nobody ought to read while he was talking and
the wife that nobody ought to talk while she was reading."
—*Vera Brittain*

"Parents have too little respect for their children,
just as the children have too much for the parents."
—*Ivy Compton-Burnett*

"In a perfect union the man and the woman
are like a strung bow.
Who is to say whether the string bends the bow,
or the bow tightens the string?"
—*Cyril Connolly*

"The value of marriage is not that adults produce children,
but that children produce adults."
—*Peter De Vries*

"My dear Watson, you as a medical man are continually
gaining lights as to the tendencies of a child
by the study of the parents.
Don't you see that the converse is equally valid?
I have frequently gained my first real insight
into the character of parents
by studying their children."
—*Arthur Conan Doyle,*
Holmes speaking

"Is not marriage an open question,
when it is alleged, from the beginning of the world,
that such as are in the institution wish to get out,
and such as are out wish to get in?"
—*Ralph Waldo Emerson*

"Men do not know their wives well;
but wives know their husbands perfectly."
—*Raoul-Auger Feuillet*

"If a guy says my wife and I
are going through a trial separation,
this inevitably refers to a separation
that will end in a trial."
—*Bruce Feirstein*

"They that marry where they do not love,
will love where they do not marry."
—*Thomas Fuller*

"Residents of the East like to point out that
people in the West fall in love and then get married,
whereas Orientals get married and then fall in love."
—*Ernest Havemann*

"Why didn't children ever see that
they could damage and harm their parents
as much as parents could damage and harm children?"
—*Laura Z. Hobson*

"It is easier for a father to have children
than for children to have a real father."
—*Pope John XXIII*

"Love is moral without legal marriage,
but marriage is immoral without love."
—*Ellen Key*

"Depression causes divorce as often as
divorce causes depression."
—*Dr. Peter Kramer*

"Direct your efforts
more to preparing youth for the path
and less to preparing the path for youth."
—*Ben Lindsey*

"Women do generally manage to love the guys they marry
more than they manage to marry the guys they love."
—*Clare Boothe Luce*

"It may be compared to a cage,
the birds without try desperately to get in,
and those within try desperately to get out."
—*Michel de Montaigne,*
on marriage

"The great secret of successful marriage is
to treat all disasters as incidents
and none of the incidents as disasters."
—*Sir Harold Nicolson*

"Adoption is not about finding children for families,
it's about finding families for children."
—*Joyce Maguire Pavao*

"After a few years of marriage
a man can look right at a woman without seeing her and
a woman can see right through a man without looking at him."
—*Helen Rowland*

"Some pray to marry the man they love,
My prayer will somewhat vary:
I humbly pray to Heaven above
That I love the man I marry."
—*Rose Pastor Stokes*

"One advantage of marriage, it seems to me,
is that when you fall out of love with him,
or he falls out of love with you,
it keeps you together until you maybe fall in love again."
—*Judith Viorst*

"Nowadays, all the married men live like bachelors,
and all the bachelors like married men."
—*Oscar Wilde*

"Before I got married
I had six theories about bringing up children;
now I have six children, and no theories."
—*John Wilmot,*
Earl of Rochester

"Most marriage failures
are caused by failures marrying."
—*Henny Youngman*

CHAPTER 14

Chiastic Insights from Great Philosophers

IN THEIR SEARCH for answers to the most important questions of life, philosophers have found a friend in chiasmus—to offer ethical insights, express paradox, make fine distinctions, and lead curious minds to deeper levels of understanding.

In the third century B.C. the Chinese philosopher Chuang-tzu awoke from a dream and made an observation that raised profound questions about what is real:

> "Once upon a time I dreamed that I was a butterfly. . . .
> Suddenly I awakened and there I lay, myself again.
> Now I do not know
> whether I was then a man dreaming I was a butterfly,
> or whether I am now a butterfly dreaming I am a man."

The seventeenth-century French philosopher Blaise Pascal put the universality of man at the heart of this piece of chiastic wisdom:

"If a laborer were to dream for twelve hours every night
that he was a king,
I believe he would be almost as happy
as a king who should dream for twelve hours every night
that he was a laborer."

And in the mid-1700s Voltaire used the subtlety of chiasmus to wonder about who created who:

"If God created us in his own image
we have more than reciprocated."

Philosophers have made of chiasmus much more than a literary or rhetorical device; they push beyond the idea of wordplay to achieve a penetrating play of ideas.

———————

"The coward calls the brave man rash,
the rash man calls him a coward."
—*Aristotle*

"If a man will begin with certainties,
he shall end in doubts;
but if he will be content to begin with doubts,
he shall end in certainties."
—*Francis Bacon*

"They that are serious in ridiculous things
will be ridiculous in serious affairs."
—*Cato the Elder*

"It is as hard for the good to suspect evil
as it is for the evil to suspect good."
—Cicero

"One man means as much to me as a multitude,
and a multitude only as much as one man."
—Democritus

"You should punish your appetites
rather than allow your appetites to punish you."
—Epictetus

"It is impossible to live pleasurably
without living wisely, well, and justly;
and impossible to live wisely, well, and justly
without living pleasurably."
—Epicurus

"One must destroy one's adversaries'
seriousness with laughter,
and their laughter with seriousness."
—Gorgias

"Anger is momentary madness,
so control your passion
or it will control you."
—Horace

"He is happy whose circumstances suit his temper
but he is more excellent who
can suit his temper to any circumstances."
—*David Hume*

"Geniuses are commonly believed to excel other men
in their power of sustained attention. . . .
But it is their genius making them attentive,
not their attention making geniuses of them."
—*William James*

"Suicide is not abominable because God prohibits it;
God prohibits it because it is abominable."
—*Immanuel Kant*

"Failure is the foundation of success;
success is the lurking place of failure."
—*Lao-tzu*

"You go without sleep to study philosophy;
on the contrary, you ought to
study philosophy to learn how to sleep."
—*Baron de Montesquieu*

"Which is it, is man one of God's blunders,
or is God one of man's blunders?"
—*Friedrich Nietzsche*

"There are only two kinds of men:
the just who believe themselves sinners;
the sinners who believe themselves just."
—*Blaise Pascal*

"Every king springs from a race of slaves,
and every slave has had kings among his ancestors."
—*Plato*

"We have, in fact, two kinds of morality side by side;
one which we preach but do not practice,
and another which we practice but seldom preach."
—*Bertrand Russell*

"It is a curious fact that in bad days
we can vividly recall the good time that is past;
but in good days we have only
a very cold and imperfect memory of the bad."
—*Arthur Schopenhauer*

"A friend is one who loves you;
but one who loves you isn't necessarily your friend."
—*Seneca the Younger*

"Remember that pain has this most excellent quality:
if prolonged it cannot be severe,
and if severe, it cannot be prolonged."
—*Seneca the Younger*

"Fear cannot be without some hope
nor hope without some fear."
—*Baruch Spinoza*

"Every abuse ought to be reformed
unless the reform is more dangerous than the abuse itself."
—*Voltaire*

"The art of progress is to preserve order amid change,
and to preserve change amid order."
—*Alfred North Whitehead*

CHAPTER 15

Chiastic Repartee

THROUGHOUT HISTORY quick-thinking wits have used chiasmus to frame crushing comebacks. In the fourth century B.C. the Greek philosopher Diogenes preached the virtues of the simple life. One of his contemporaries was a worldly philosopher named Aristippus, a sycophant who secured a cushy position in the king's court by currying favor with the emperor. One day, as Diogenes was preparing lentils for his simple evening meal, the cocky court philosopher arrived on the scene and announced: "If you would only learn to flatter the king, you wouldn't have to live on lentils."

Diogenes' response is the stuff of legend:

> "If you would only learn to live on lentils,
> you wouldn't have to flatter the king."

With the right setup, chiastic repartee can be impossible to resist. A perfect example occurs in a memorable conversation in *For*

Whom the Bell Tolls. Discussing cowardice, Pablo says to Anselmo, "It is not cowardly to know what is foolish." Hemingway sees an opportunity to craft one of his "double *dichos*" and writes:

> " 'Neither is it foolish to know what is cowardly,'
> said Anselmo, unable to resist making the phrase."

A modern-day example comes from a longtime female resident of Alaska, asked by a new arrival: "What are the chances of finding a good man around here?" There was a pause. Alaska was full of men. But would she recommend any of them? The old-timer replied:

> "Well, the odds are good,
> but the goods are odd."

The saying has since become an in-joke among women in every part of the world who see the truth of the observation regardless of the number of men who are available.

> "Has running added years to my life?
> No, but it's added life to my years."
> —*Anonymous Boston Marathon runner,*
> age seventy-five

> "God is dead." — Nietzsche
> "Nietzsche is dead." — God
> —*Anonymous graffiti*

An English lord introduced two bills in Parliament, one protecting badgers, the other reforming laws regarding homosexuality. When one of his peers was asked how he'd characterize his lordship's legislative interests, the gentleman replied:

"Teaching people not to bugger badgers
and not to badger buggers."

◆

When a friend asked J. M. Barrie about a speech he gave at Smith College, the shy writer replied:

"To tell you the truth,
I'd much rather talk one thousand times to one girl
than talk one time to a thousand girls."

◆

Arriving at church one Sunday morning, the preacher Henry Ward Beecher found an anonymous letter in his mailbox containing a single word: *Fool!* In his sermon that morning, he said:

"I have known many an instance of a man writing a letter
and forgetting to sign his name,
but this is the only instance I have ever known of
a man signing his name
and forgetting to write the letter."

◆

In 1980 Vassar College named William F. Buckley the commencement speaker. A majority of the graduating seniors signed a petition protesting the selection. Buckley withdrew, but not before offering this parting shot:

"The majority of the senior class at Vassar does not
desire my company and I must confess,
having read specimens of their thought and sentiments,
that I do not desire
the company of the majority of the senior class of Vassar."

◆

After Kim Campbell, the first female prime minister of Canada, appeared bare-shouldered at a banquet, opponents criticized her for emulating Madonna. Asked about it at a press conference, she replied:

"A comparison between Madonna and me is a comparison
between a strapless evening gown
and a gownless evening strap."

◆

Sharper: "'Thus grief still treads upon the heels of pleasure:
Marry'd in haste, we may repent at leisure"

Setter: "Some by experience find those words misplac'd:
At leisure marry'd, they repent in haste."

— *William Congreve,*
in *The Old Bachelor* (1693)

When Vladimir Horowitz asked Pablo Casals about the secret of his success, Casals replied:

"You have to play Mozart like Chopin
and Chopin like Mozart."

◆

To someone who complained about his drinking, Winston Churchill commented:

"All I can say is that
I have taken more out of alcohol
than alcohol has taken out of me."

To a friend who said, "Winston! How wonderfully your new grandson resembles you," Churchill said:

"All babies look like me.
But then, I look like all babies."

◆

Visiting Mahatma Gandhi, the artist Jo Davidson brought along photos of his sculpture. Gandhi examined them intently and said, "I see you make heroes out of mud." The sculptor replied:

"And sometimes vice versa."

◆

A popular after-dinner speaker, Chauncey Depew was introduced by an emcee who said, "Chauncey Depew can always produce a speech. All you have to do is give him his dinner, and up comes his speech." In his opening remarks, Depew delighted the audience by saying:

"I only hope that it isn't true that if I give you my speech,
up will come your dinner."

◆

Asked to explain his theory of relativity in layman's terms, Albert Einstein replied:

"When a man sits with a pretty girl for an hour,
it seems like a minute.
But let him sit on a hot stove for a minute —
and it's longer than any hour."

◆

"I heard an answer today to the platitude:
'There's no money in poetry.'
It was: 'There's no poetry in money, either.' "
— *Robert Graves*

Edward Everett Hale was asked, "As Senate chaplain, do you look at the condition of the country and then pray that the Almighty will give Senators the wisdom to deal with these problems?" He replied:

"I do not look at the country and pray for the Senators.
I look at the Senators and pray for the country."

◆

In Mel Brooks's 1994 *Robin Hood: Men in Tights*, Robin (Carey Elwes) is taken to a dungeon and locked in chains alongside another prisoner (Isaac Hayes). After the following chiastic dialogue, they press their feet against the iron bar holding them, breaking free.

Robin Hood: "It's not going to be easy getting out of here.
What we need is a great feat of strength."

Prisoner: "Feat of strength? *Au contraire.*
Now that you are here with me,
what we have is great strength of feet."

◆

Asked if he took naps, Dr. Samuel Johnson replied:

"I never take a nap after dinner
but when I have had a bad night,
and then the nap takes me."

During the Civil War a White House visitor said to Abraham
Lincoln, "God is on our side." Lincoln replied:

"We trust, sir, that God is on our side.
It is more important to know that we are on God's side."

◆

Robert Dale Owen, a prominent spiritualist, asked Lincoln's
opinion about an article on spiritualism. Not wanting to be rude,
Lincoln said:

"Well, for those who like that sort of thing I should think
that is just the sort of thing they should like."

◆

"I once asked Edwin Arlington Robinson
if he did not think his sense of humor had lengthened his life.
'I think,' he replied, 'my life has lengthened my sense of humor.'"
—*Daniel Gregory Mason*

A wealthy patron commissioned Michelangelo to do a sculpture
and then complained that the sculptor was taking far too long to
make only trifling changes in the piece. The artist replied:

"Trifles make perfection,
and perfection is no trifle."

◆

"Some of the guards . . . came out, and they said:
'Why did you break our windows? We have done nothing.'
She said: 'It is because
you have done nothing I have broken your windows.'"
—*Emmeline Pankhurst,*
quoting a woman jailed for her suffrage activities

Explaining how Soviet leaders pressured him to decline the
Nobel Prize in 1958, Boris Pasternak said:

"They don't ask much of you.
They only want you to hate the things you love
and love the things you despise."

◆

Kristin Scott-Thomas: "I hear you help people
with horse problems."
Robert Redford: "The truth is I help horses
with people problems."
—from *The Horse Whisperer* (1998)

Chief Justice: "Your means are very slender,
and your waste is great."
Falstaff: "I would it were otherwise.
I would my means were greater
and my waist slenderer."
—*William Shakespeare,*
in *King Henry IV, Part Two*

The dancer Isadora Duncan, a big believer in eugenics, was en-amored of George Bernard Shaw and thought a child between them would be quite a specimen. She said to him, "Think of it! With my body and your brains, what a wonder it would be!" He replied:

"Yes, but what if it had your brains and my body?"

◆

The English writer Richard Brinsley Sheridan was forever in debt. His tailor, tired of asking Sheridan to pay his bill, pleaded, "At least you could pay me the interest on the principal." Sheri-dan replied:

"It is not my interest to pay the principal;
nor is it my principle to pay the interest."

◆

CHAPTER 16

Implied Chiasmus

EARLY IN HIS CAREER, the struggling young writer George Bernard Shaw submitted a play to a well-known London producer, who flatly rejected it. Several years later, the same producer sent a telegram to Shaw—now a successful playwright—saying he was, after all, interested in producing the work. Shaw cabled his reply:

"Better never than late."

This is a brilliant example of *implied chiasmus*, a term I've coined to describe a special kind of abbreviated chiastic expression. Ordinarily chiasmus contains two phrases or clauses, the second one reversing the first. In implied chiasmus a reversal implies a saying—generally a well-known one—but stands alone. The technique has been used to great effect by world-class wits, as in Mae West's signature line, "A hard man is good to find."

Some great examples come from headline and caption writers. A few years ago *Sports Illustrated* ran a photograph of the official timers at a track meet. The caption at the bottom of the photo was brilliant:

> "These are the souls that time men's tries."

As it turns out, I'm not the only admirer of implied chiasmus. In 1983, the captain of the USS *Enterprise* grounded his ship on a sandbar in San Francisco Bay. Herb Caen of the *San Francisco Chronicle* marveled over the comment of one Bay-area wit:

> "He grounds the warship he walks on."

The fun of implied chiasmus is dual. First you have the pleasure of figuring out what's been reversed; then you get to marvel over the ingenuity behind these inspired chiastic creations.

———

> "Time wounds all heels."
> —*Jane Sherwood Ace*

> "The best lives of our years."
> —*Advertising slogan*
> for A&E's *Biography* series

> "You can tell a lot about a company by the people they keep."
> —*Advertising slogan*
> for Microsoft Corporation

"A hangover is the wrath of grapes."
—Anonymous

"He snatched defeat from the jaws of victory."
—Anonymous,
originally about Thomas E. Dewey in 1948

"Clearly the moral of this extravaganza
is to leave no stern untoned!"
—Anonymous critic,
on a Broadway show featuring a cast's well-toned derrieres

"Think of us as ships deserting a sinking rat."
—Robert Benchley,
on leaving *Vanity Fair* magazine

When the Company Theatre of Norwell, Massachusetts, had trouble getting permission to perform a stage version of Stephen King's thriller *Misery,* artistic director Zoe Bradford decided to call King directly. He immediately granted permission after hearing her say:

"Company loves *Misery.*"

◆

"Don't look now, Tallulah, but your show is slipping."
—*Heywood Broun,*
to Tallulah Bankhead,
after a disappointing performance

"Gluttony is an emotional escape,
a sign something is eating us."
—*Peter De Vries*

"My old drama coach used to say,
'Don't just do something, stand there.'"
—*Clint Eastwood*

"It was a brilliant affair;
water flowed like champagne."
—*William M. Evarts,*
on a White House dinner given
by Rutherford B. Hayes,
a temperance advocate

"Time's fun when you're having flies."
—*Kermit the Frog* (*Jim Henson*)

"Only the young die good."
—*Oliver Herford*

"Some things have to be
believed to be seen."
—*Ralph Hodgson*

"An honest God is the noblest work of man."
—*Robert G. Ingersoll,*
reversing Alexander Pope

"Gone today, here tomorrow."
—*Alfred Knopf,*
on books returned to publishers

"Last guys don't finish nice."
—*Allen L. Otten*

"I never liked a man I didn't meet."
—*Dorothy Parker*

"It's a great place to live,
but I wouldn't want to visit there."
— Will Rogers,
on Hollywood

A *Saturday Night Live* parody of a popular U.S. Navy recruiting
commercial showed a frustrated sailor scrubbing floors, cleaning
latrines, and performing other menial duties. The tag line said:

"It's not just an adventure, it's a job."

◆

"A drama critic is a man who leaves no turn unstoned."
— George Bernard Shaw

"A race track is a place where windows clean people."
— Danny Thomas

"Greater love hath no man than this,
that he lay down his friends for his life."
— Jeremy Thorpe,
after Harold Macmillan fired
seven members of his cabinet in 1962

"Invention is the mother of necessity."
— Thorstein Veblen

"Reality is a crutch for people who can't cope with drugs."
— Jane Wagner and Lily Tomlin

"The English have a miraculous power
of turning wine into water."
—*Oscar Wilde*

"Work is the curse of the drinking classes."
—*Oscar Wilde*

"Who am I to stone the first cast?"
—*Walter Winchell,*
on his tendency to praise
opening Broadway shows

"A broker is a man who takes your fortune
and runs it into a shoestring."
—*Alexander Woollcott*

"The waist is a terrible thing to mind."
—*Ziggy (Tom Wilson)*

INDEX

WITHDRAWAL